# South Western Designs

## A coloring book for the not so very young.

## Artwork by J. A. Christensen

Dedicated to:

My friend and mentor
Ms. Kimberly

Also available: *Mandalas of the Southwest*: An adult coloring book for fun and relaxation.
(Amazon and CreateSpace)

See these designs (and others) on products at:
www.zazzle.com/goathilldesigns
www.etsy.com/GoatHillCreations

Contact me at: goathillcreations@gmail.com

or follow at
**www.facebook.com/goathillcreations**
or to view these designs, upcoming coloring art and coloring ideas.

Watch for next edition!

Enjoy

Goat Hill Designs
by
"jud" aka J. A, Christensen

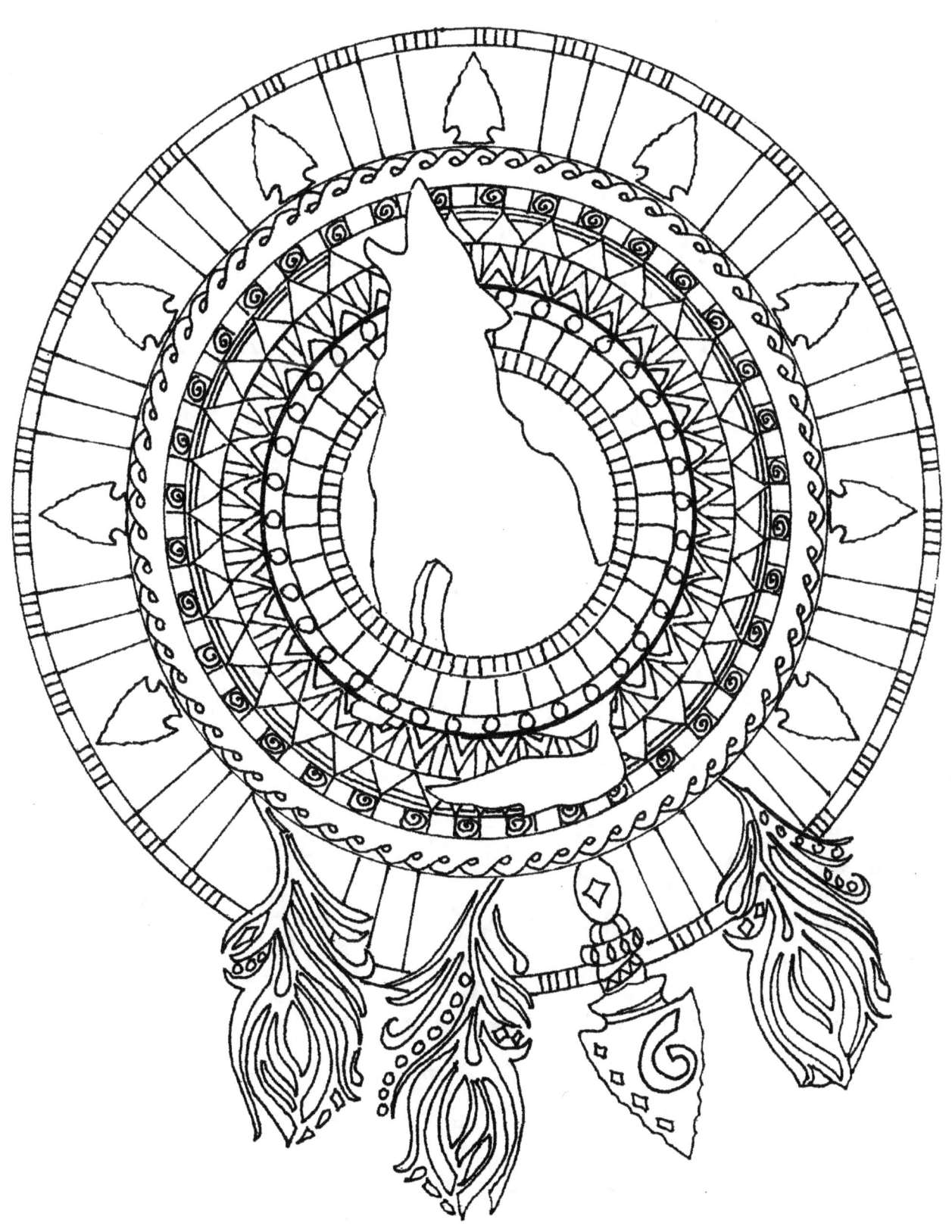

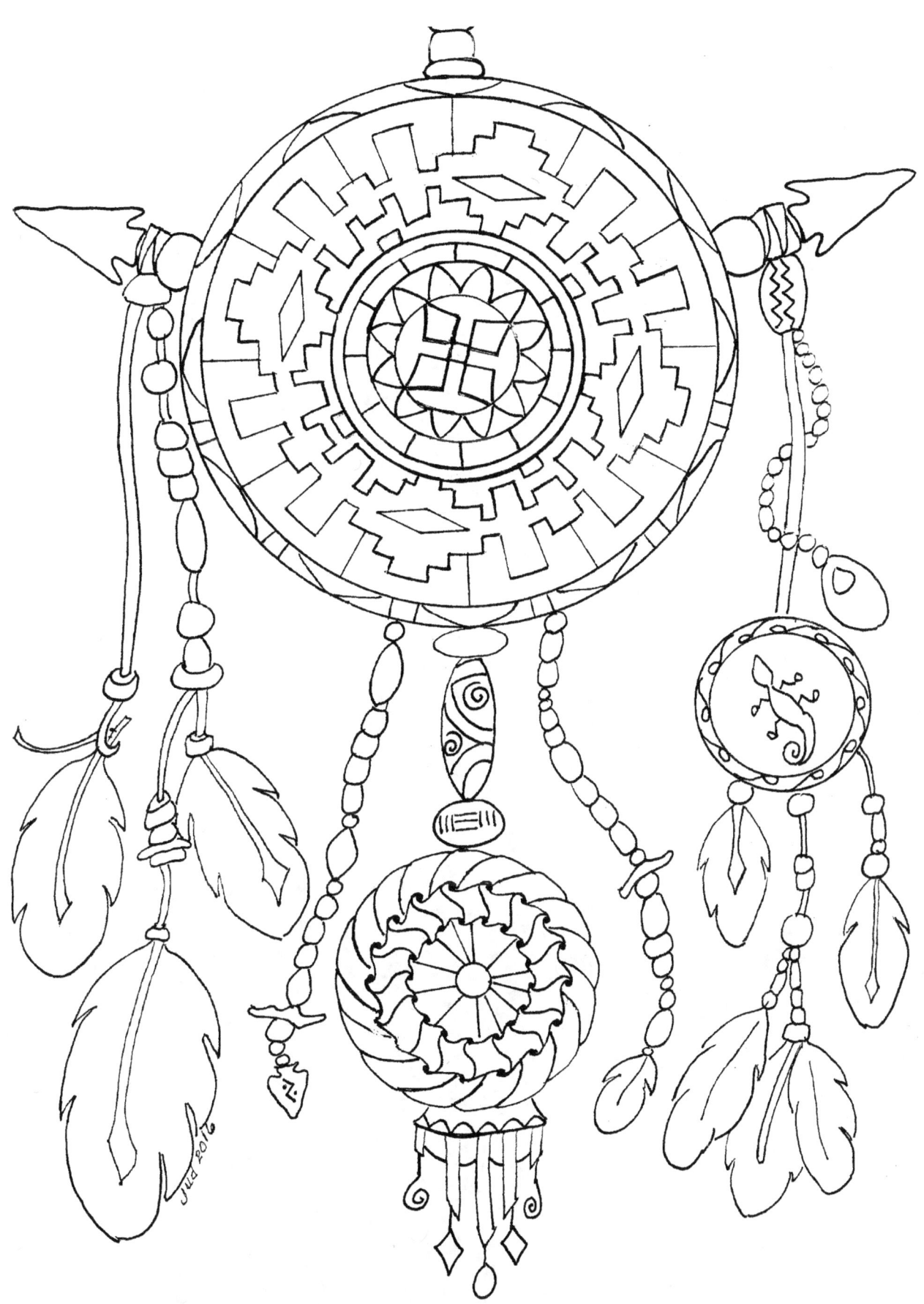

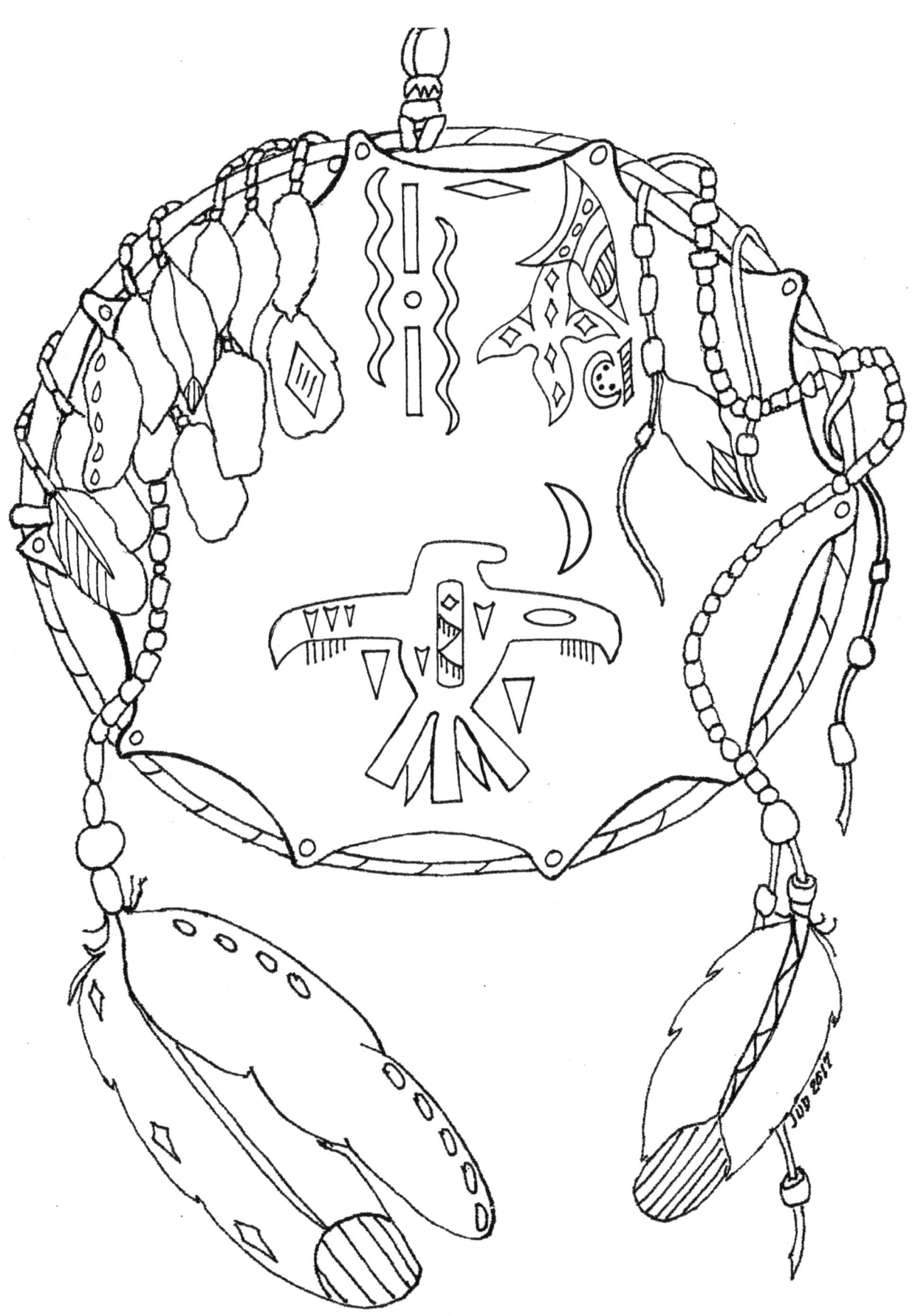

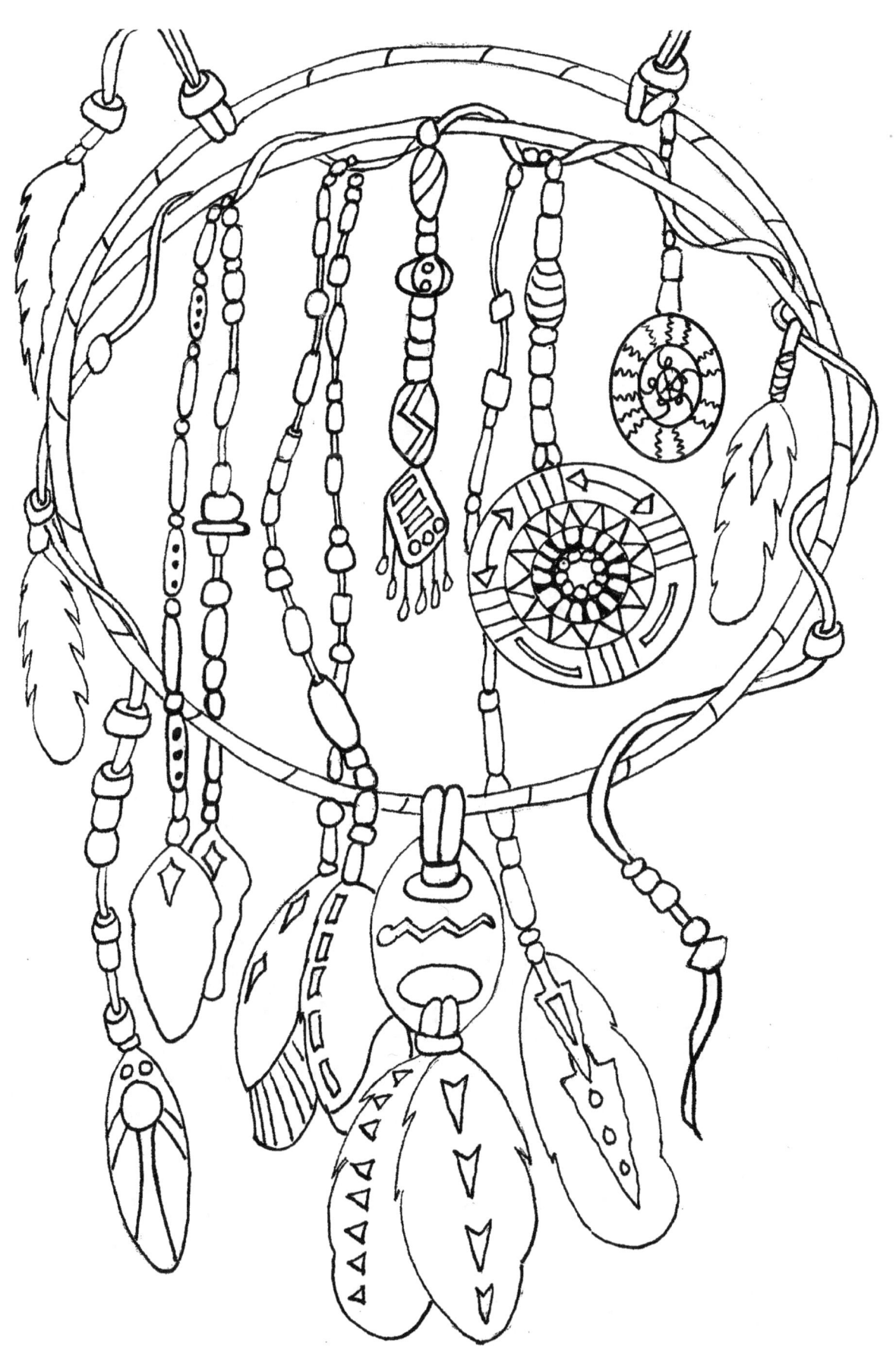